HOW TO BE A SHARK SALESMAN?

RITESH MOHAN

First Published in April 2022

ISBN: 978-93-93899-07-1

BLUEROSE PUBLISHERS

www.bluerosepublishers.com

info@bluerosepublishers.com

+91 8882 898 898

Cover Design:

Akash Bartwal

Typographic Design:

Ilma

Distributed by: BlueRose, Amazon, Flipkart

Dedication

This Book has been dedicated to all those people who have inspired me to become a Thought Leader in the Retail sector.

I dedicate this book to all my managers in the corporate world who gave me an opportunity to learn the craft of SALES both in FMCG & Retail sectors.

I would have not done justice, if these industry stalwarts would have not supported me by mentoring me to walk through the corporate ladder and learn the art of selling- which happens to be a bloodline for any business.

I would like to thank my first boss Mr. Eric Menezes, Chairman of Menezes cosmetics Pvt Ltd (a part of CMM group of companies) who taught me the value of hard work and creative thinking.

Mr. Nalin Bhandari (former Business Head of DS Group), Mr Hisham almoudi, CEO, KOJ Est, Mr. Kamal Osman Jamjoom, Chairman of KOJ Est,

Last but not the least a big hug and love to my loving mother, Mrs. Indu Saxena whose blessings have helped me become an author.

Thanks to my support system – My wife Megha who has selflessly dedicated herself to take care of my two kids and has been keeping the family together.

A special mention for my lovely daughter Mehak and son Raunak for their unconditional love.

A big gratitude to my extended family in New Delhi & Dehradun (my cousin brothers and sisters) for always supporting & loving me (Me being the youngest in the joint family).

Introduction

The Book is all about Sales Management.

In today's digital era, everyone is selling to each other.

Employee selling his skills to his employer,

Entrepreneurs are selling their ideas to Venture capitalists,

Boy friend selling his aspirations and dreams to his girlfriend & kids are selling to their parents and vice versa.

Hence we all are in SELLING Business.

If we agree that we all are in Selling business then we need to learn and acquire selling skills to grow within our industry.

Gone are the days when a chartered accountant used to say, I am not into sales.

Today right from CEO of an organization to the lowest rank is in Sales Business.

My book, " How to become a shark salesman" provides tricks, concepts and hacks to grow your business by learning the Art of selling & become a "Shark" in selling.

The title of the book has been inspired from the International television series called " Shark Tank" which promotes the concept of entrepreneurship.

There are **25 chapters** in the book which are inspired from my real life experiences for over 24 years in Retail sales and Marketing.

The Book covers topic from the basic sales tenets to selling in digital era and covers briefly about the importance of Leadership in sales.

The style of the book is simple and lucid.

I have tried my best to provide the real-life cases & examples for easy grasping of the concept and hacks.

Hope everyone of you will find this book useful and will grow your sales careers.

Love

Ritesh Mohan aka Retail Ritesh.

Contents

Chapter 1

We are all part of 4 seconds generation.

Selling is a process between a seller and a customer. A process which builds trust between seller and customers.

Trust is the most important virtue that every salesman need to strive for in order to earn trust amongst his/her customers.

In digital age, this process has become too time-bound and challenging.

How?

Today in age of smartphones, social media, our attention span has reduced drastically and we tend to swipe to next post or content which is not relevant to us.

It take 3-4 secs only to swipe to alternative content.

Customers today are spoilt for choices and is true in case of branded content and products.

As the businesses move online, it is pertinent that every salesman should strive to grab his customers attention in less than 3 secs, otherwise the opportunity to sell is gone.

The window for grabbing customer's attention is only 3-4secs.

It is challenging for sales & marketeers to act positively in 3secs to engage their clients so swiftly.

Qualities for a shark salesman to imbibe in digital age are:

- Know your customer's preferences and Buying behaviour.
- Create your sales funnel for reaching out to your customers and engaging them with your brand.
- Feed them with relevant contextual content, 'don't sell immediately'
- Keep adapting your sales techniques and funnel regularly.

Let me explain each one separately.

Know your customer's preferences and Buying behaviour:

A shark salesman creates his/her Buyer's persona based on the historical sales experience. Use digital social media platforms like Facebook to create "look alike" audience and reach similar buyers through digital channels.

Monitor and subscribe to tools like Google trends to keep yourself updated as to what's happening in your sector and how can you benefit from it.

Understanding customers are no longer prerogative of Marketing department but everyone in the business need to study and monitor customer's buying patterns and preferences.

Insight- Everyone of us are born salesman, we are selling everyday i.e. a child is selling his idea to his parents so that they can buy him a toy, you are selling yourself to your girlfriend with gifts etc, to win her over. Each one of us are directly or indirectly involved in sales.

Create your sales funnel for reaching out to your customers and engaging them with your brand.

This is 3 step process:

- Build awareness – bringing your brand or product, service in front of prospects.
- Get your brand into consideration set – Highlight the problem your prospect is facing and then help him out with your solution or service/product.
- Call to action – sell the problem, the solution will sell itself.

Feed them with relevant contextual content, 'don't sell immediately'

Shark salesmen always seek the right questions

Observe and learn about

- How is your buyer's purchase journey?
- When did they visit your store or online ecommerce site.
- Which page or which section did they dwell most of the time.

Understand their buying cycle and ask relevant questions to make their journey more seamless.

Engaging your prospects by contextual content aimed at resolving his/her business problems will help you build Trust.

Keep adapting your sales funnel till you start getting desired results.

Social selling skill – a must-have for the shark salesman.

Selling in the digital age means higher expectations regardless of selling in the B2C or B2B space.

It means your prospects are making decisions about you and your services long before they ever make contact with you or a fellow sales rep.

This makes personalization even more challenging but all the more necessary in order to stand out among your competitors.

Consider these statistics:

- 65% of business buyers say they'd switch brands if a company didn't make efforts to personalize their communications.

- 75% of business buyers expect companies to anticipate their needs and make relevant suggestions by the year 2020.
- Personalized emails deliver 6x higher transaction rates.
- 75% of consumers are more likely to buy from a retailer that recognizes them by name, recommends options based on past purchases, OR knows their purchase history.

Social selling is about building a connection with your audience before they buy your product or service.

Always remember we have 4 seconds to make an impact or lose customer forever.

Chapter 2

Getting Better at closing a sale - Transactional vs Relationship building.

Do you take pride in Selling or being in the sales profession?

The general perception pertaining the sales job or sales profile is negative. People try to shy away from this profession just because they are driven by perceptions of others.

"What will my neighbor or my friend say or think about me", "Was he not good to get into some respectable profession"

These kinds of fears keep a common salesman mediocre.

The reality is completely different, Sales is the only profession wherein the employee decides his own paycheck. (Commissions are endless).

It is one of the highly paid professions.

What is selling?

Selling is nothing but the transfer of enthusiasm from seller to buyer.

Enthusiasm comes from having strong belief in his product or service. A shark salesman will always put himself in his customer shoes.

If he is not ready to buy from his own money, his own product then he has no right to sell it also.

A strong conviction is required which only comes if you are passionate about you are doing and you know your business and product inside-out.

Selling is 90% conviction & 10% communication of the conviction.

In one of the luxury brands that I was handling and selling fragrances which were niche and ultra-niche luxury fragrances; we noticed that our salespeople lacked the convincing power and one of the reasons was that they had never used such a hi-end, expensive product earlier.

As a business, we took a call to allocate one fragrance bottle of their choice, each to every salesman so that they wear it and experience the delight and individuality that fragrance brings out in the person.

Our sales results were very positive and encouraging as the sales personnel started selling more convincingly, more confidence oozed out from their sales pitches.

Gifting One fragrance bottle had changed the entire game for us.

Remember, Shark salesman compete against themselves; they better their own records constantly.

There are 3 types of selling methodologies

- Transactional - Get the sale, at all costs.
- The focus is on winning this one sale without much thought to the customer's needs or the longer-term.
- Sales relationship is purely transaction based.
- Relationship based selling – its built on Trust.
- Relational selling is about building long-term relationships. The sales rep gets to know their customer, their needs, and their wants.

Both approaches to selling can be effective, but if you're looking to go beyond just making a sale, and you want to retain customers and build strong relationships, then the focus must be on relational selling.

For Instance, if you are selling beauty products, you can do sampling and push the women to buy your products by listing Product's Unique selling propositions and benefits, that's what most of the salespeople do in their jobs. That's call transactional selling as your objective is to sell.

In relationship-based selling, You do the above but before explaining the women the product benefits, you ask questions.

Questions about why she is looking for beauty products, what kind of products has she been using, what are the problems or issues faced by her currently using different brands. And only on listening to her pain points, you suggest your products or even go a step further by handing out the sampling sachets of your products and asking the women to try it out prior to making her purchase decision.

Here your objective is not immediate sales but building a connect with the women customer so that she tries your sample and upon liking it, she buys it. In return of the sample, you collect her email or contact details and use this data for your retargeting marketing exercises.

- Consultative selling or Diagnostic selling.

This is the most advised form of selling.

Consultative selling is a more complex, long-term process that involves collaboration between the buyer and seller.

Consider it like your family doctor.

Upon visiting your doctor, the doctor first greets you and ask you about your family welfare before coming to you.

He asks questions to determine what the issue is, which you are currently facing.

Investigate as to how long you have been having these issues, investigate the cause of the illness by doing some tests.

Basically, he tries to reach the root cause of the illness prior to prescribing the medicine or solutions.

Similarly in consultative selling, the salesperson must know more about their product or services to offer solutions in order to guide their customers.

Salesperson should be well trained not only with he/she is selling but also with what is happening in the industry in the world.

Consultative selling makes the shark salesman as an Authority and builds a strong bond.

The interaction becomes more of a relationship than a transaction.

Benefits of Consultative selling

- Turns you and your team into professional problem solvers
- Gives long-term solutions to your customers
- Builds long-term relationships with your customers
- Produces customized solutions vs. generic solutions

- Builds trust in you and your brand

Shark salesman vs traditional salesman

Do not think of yourself as a salesperson.

Instead, consider yourself a consultant/ authority or problem-solver.

It is not your job to sell your product or your service;

it's your job to help the customer find the right solution.

If your goal is to help the customer instead of closing a sale, you will build customer loyalty because they know they can trust your advice.

Customer loyalty equals long-term sales.

Ask Questions

The best consultative selling technique is to **ASK QUESTIONS** to discover how you can best *serve* your client or prospective customer.

By doing so, you can personalize the solution based on your client's needs.

Even if the solution does not result to immediate sales but it will help you become a trusted advisor in the eyes of the customer & the customer shall return to you whenever he/she needs any advice.

Put the customers into Spotlight/ Give them importance.

Every customer wants to be listened, wants to be appreciated or heard rather than being pushed by the salesman.

Shark salesmen imbibe the qualities of "active listening" and "asking the right persuasive questions".

One of my friends, who works in a leading Big 5 management firms, told me, his work was largely about helping his clients do what they already know they should do.

So the consultative selling is really a collaborative effort to begin identifying enough about the company's pain to be able to detect some potential causes, and test them.

Note to shark salesmen:

Selling is a rejection business; you get more NO's then Yes's.

Code your mind to decode NO as "Next Opportunity." Being resilient is the key to becoming a shark salesman. The more will be touched upon in the next chapter.

Chapter 3

Characteristics of a shark salesman

Many sales people need to take steps to get people to give them their undivided attention.

If you are in B2B selling then the first challenge is to get an appointment from your customer.

The first main characteristics of a shark salesman is "Unconventional approach" i.e. they don't shy from trying out unconventional way to seek attention of their customers.

I tried couple of hacks during my sales days wherein I was responsible for running a post-production & animation studio and my main customers were the big advertising agencies.

To get through the creative head or the production head was a big challenge itself.

I used to visit their offices during morning tea breaks and used to carry a dozen of donuts from the nearest bakery (fresh-baked donuts) and used to hand over to the receptionist asking them that it is courtesy from my company.

As a result, I was able to put forth my agency's name in front of the agency's workers and got a time to network with them prior to even fixing a meeting.

Moreover, I used to become friendly with the front office desk employees, who used to guide me to the exact responsible person by doing a soft introduction to the agency's creative directors.

Point to remember:

"Think about how your customers' business work and aim to fit in with their special nature".

In second chapter, we have talked about transactional relationship vs diagnostic relationships, the one of the main characteristics of a shark salesman is " to earn trust & respect" of his customers.

He needs to become a "go-to source" for the customer whenever they need any of his services.

If a customer sees you as a professional, they will be more likely to trust you, to listen to your advice and to buy from you.

Sales and service always overlap.

Another characteristic of a shark salespeople is that they provide delightful service.

During one of my work visit to Bahrain, I checked into one of the hotels and there was a gentleman, who greeted me and asked me if I had a prior booking.

I told him yes, I had booked the room through an online booking site and showed him the QR code.

He immediately scanned the code and address me by my first name and completed the check-in formalities very efficiently while I waited in the lounge and sipped my welcome drink.

He came to me and gave me the keys and my passport and told me that as a special gesture the hotel has offered me a free complimentary airport drop taxi for me for my next day travel out of the country.

I loved the courtesy and the gesture from the front office and what impressed me more was the business acumen of the front office personnel, he saw me as a frequent business traveler and ensured that he delights me with the hotel's services so that I can always continue staying with them during my visits to Bahrain.

And how true this front office gentleman was, I always stayed with the same hotel whenever I visited Bahrain and loved the way the hotel kept treating their frequent customers.

Points to remember

Delight your customers with world class service that builds the bond.

Become a go-to person for your customers whenever he needs any of your services. Building trust and respect is the core characteristics of a shark salesman.

Chapter 4

Be visible and Available

Be Visible and Available.

Selling is the overall part of marketing efforts.

Marketing generates awareness and interest for your brand or business, and it is the sales responsibility to convert that interest into purchase or sale.

Out of sight, out of mind – an old proverb.

Personal branding is the most effective tool to build yours and your brand's visibility and in turn earn some trust amongst your customers and prospects.

In chapter 2 we had talked about social selling skills, the usage of social media can definitely boost your visibility and generate trust.

People always ask me,

"Is over exposure or visibility Bad?"

My reply, over exposure/ Visibility is never bad.

Coca Cola, known by almost everyone on the planet Earth. You can find it across every store on every shelf, hotels, pubs, restaurants, gaming alleys.

Is it over exposed or over visible?

Answer is definitely NO.

Point to remember

Build your brand (including your Personal Brand) so BIG & LARGE that people stand in admiration of your ability to take actions and build a scalable business.

The best way to silent your critics is by showing your success.

We have seen the CEO of Xiaomi India Mr Manu kumar Jain, who is a well know corporate leader and has built his personal brand so strong that today brand like Xiaomi is leveraging his personal brand to explore new domains of the businesses.

Xiaomi phones were the first one to use ISRO's (India's elite satellite organization) first navigational tool which is faster than google maps.

Being more visible and available to your customers will help you avoid the most common answer that the customers give,

"I will let you know post thinking about it".

This sentence is as good as saying, " I don't need your services at the moment, thanks".

For most salespeople, it is the end of the sales process but for the shark salesman, it is start of the sales re-targeting process.

He would request the contact information from his prospect and use the re-targeting tools to target the prospect on his social media, build the trust by sharing the industry related news and insights on the messenger.

Salesman would utilize the down time to build interest in his prospect mind by continuing giving him information & insights that prospect's business would need.

Thus, he is building his selling pipeline for the future.

By staying in touch with his prospect, he ensured that his prospect's interest in buying his services remained active and he did not lose the customer to his competitors.

Let me share my personal experience here as well, during one of my holidays to Goa, (I had gone to complete writing my first book -simplifying retail).

I was staying in hotel Marriott (anjuna beach) and was surprised that during the breakfast on the first day, the hotel's GM personally visited every table and greeted the guest.

When he asked me the purpose of my visit to Goa, I told him that I am here to complete writing my book and was planning to spend most of the time in the hotel in writing and reading.

He gave me his personal number and asked me to call him in case I needed any assistance, and he went on instructing his team member to ensure that my room is fully equipped with coffee and water, and he gave me the access to the hotel's printer in case I wanted to print any of my manuscripts.

This small gesture not only earned my respect for the gentleman but also loyalty for his hotel.

My lesson:

Be seen to "go the extra mile"

The most famous physics law "the inverse square law" holds perfectly in the sales management.

It states your influence on the customer is directly proportional to how close you are to the customer.

In digital age, staying close to your customer means regular emailers, newsletters, personal video conferencing, social networking etc, instant messaging etc.

$I = K/D^2$ (digit 2 is power of ^{2})

I – influence, K – constant , D- distance and 2 – power of two

Chapter 5

Be a trust-worthy partner

Winning the customer's trust is the ultimate objective of sales and it should form the ultimate single focused objective for any salesman.

I shall illustrate one hack in building trust which has been used by MNCs giants like Microsoft.

Its called Freemium technique, Microsoft used the launch of windows 10 to build trust amongst its customers by offering them free upgrade from windows 7,8 to 10.

Microsoft did not earn from windows 10 but won trust and also avoided its user base to shift to Mac operating systems.

Secondly, people using windows 10 may opt to purchase other Microsoft products like upgraded MS office etc.

Hence sometimes giving something free can build trust and also act as an entry barrier to the competition.

Another hack to build trust is to follow the **law of Reciprocity.**

We, Human beings are all pre coded to be receptive and feel obligated to reciprocate, when something is offered to us complimentary.

It is built into our system as a subconscious mind action.

I learnt this hack during my tenure with one of the local perfumery retail group.

We used to offer complimentary Arabic coffee (ghawa) to all the customers who visited our stores prior to showing any of our scents or collections.

We realized that offering of Arabic coffee is an important sales tool.

It used to help customers feel relaxed and customers used to listen to our sales pitch more patiently and it resulted in higher rate of conversions.

Building trust is one of the foremost qualities of a shark salesman.

Giving a small momento or gifts with purchase to your customers can also build brand recall and trust amongst the customers.

Though, Giving GWPs (gift with purchase) is a promotional technique but it too can lead to build trust and recall. It depends as to how the salesman uses this technique.

I recall me receiving a Gift with purchase from my favorite brand Mont Blanc on purchasing one of their limited-edition pen.

The salesman gave me a business card holder as a gift and the way he presented to me, made me felt very special- like a VVIP customer.

I still use the business card holder and it keeps reminding me of the salesman and how made me felt when I bought from Mont Blanc.

Sometimes, it is only sufficient to treat the customer nicely and with empathy to win their trust.

Even dale Carnegie, in his book," how to win friends & influence people" quoted,

"The only way on the earth to influence people is talk about what they want and show them how to get it".

The shark salesman uses this technique to the core to build trust amongst its customers.

Points to remember

Use the law of reciprocity to your advantage

Follow empathy, talk what your customers want to listen and build trust

Treat them in a way that they remember you always as to how you made them felt as a VVIP customer.

Use Freemium technique to build trust.

Chapter 6

Paper clip strategy.

It is a part of behavioral study and was first used to build strong good habits.

There are a variety of popular behavioral economics studies that refer to this as the Endowed Progress Effect, which essentially says we place more value on things once we have them.

In other words, the **more paper clips you move to the "Completed" bin**, the more valuable completing the habit becomes to you.

This strategy is going to be useful for sales professionals who are in insurance, stock broking or real estate & depend upon calling their customers regularly or even cold calling.

Mr. X, an insurance broker used to carry two empty glass jar, one filled with 120 paper clips and another empty.

He used to start making calls and post call, he used pick & drop one clip from filled jar to empty one.

He kept doing in for 6 months without breaking the chain.

By the end of six months, he was bringing approx. USD 5 million worth of business to his firm.

Making a progress is fine but making a visual representation of it i.e. moving the clip from one jar to another reinforces the clear evidence of the progress.

It is a growth hack called as paperclip strategy.

A shark salesman, uses the power of visual cues to his advantage

Visual cues display your progress on a behavior.

Everyone knows consistency is an essential component of success, but few people actually measure how consistent they are in real life.

Developing your "To Do list" daily i.e. the number of calls to be made on daily basis or number of meetings to be done daily and then follow up with the prospects regularly in order to convert the cold leads into hot leads and ultimately into sales.

Create your own paper clip strategy

- Need to send 25 sales emails/ cold calls every day? Start with 25 paper clips and toss one to the other side each time you press Send.
- Want to drink 8 glasses of water each day? Start with 8 paper clips and slide one over each time you finish a glass.

Points to remember

- Use the power of visual cues to remind you to stay on your goals or sales objectives.
- Being consistent is the key to success for shark salesman.

Chapter 7

Identify the Key Decision maker.

Selling is an art of persuasion.

You need to know not only your customer but also all the emotions & personalities that influence him or her.

Even Indian scriptures talks about this principle. In Mahabharata, every one knew that the leader of Pandavas is Yudisthir (eldest Pandavas) but in reality all the decisions were influenced by Lord Krishna.

Pandavas listened to his views and actioned the suggestions.

Shark salesmen identify who they are talking to and what role they play in decision making is very important is selling.

During my advertising stint, I have always professed one basic principle, the head of the company or the business owner should pen down the creative brief for his marketing team i.e. he needs to narrate his vision for the business, and how he needs the help of his creative team to make that vision in reality by means of creative executions.

Many times, it is seen that marketing head writes the creative brief and shares with the agency, the agency works on that brief and presents few options which are then rejected by the business owner or management.

Resulting in overall wastage of resources – people's time, efforts and creative ideas.

Identifying the key decision maker became pivotal for me during my agency days as it ensured that the correct resources were deployed, and ideas presented were in line with the key decision maker's vision.

We all know that car buying is one of the important buying decisions especially if you are buying your first family car.

The shark car salesman would not only welcome his customer to his showroom but also would arrange a test drive for you in the shortlisted vehicle.

During the test drive, asking the right question to the customer would enhance the possibility of closing the sale.

Questions like:

What is your profession? Is this car going to your first car or second car?

Deep dive into questioning and finding out the emotions and interest, that drives the buying decision etc.

A shark salesman would then be able to utilize emotional cues to close the sales.

For example- dropping off the customer post his test drive to his home and invite the family members to have a view, (especially kids).

- Parking the test car in the parking lot, provides visual cues to the prospective customer as to how the car would look in his house and boosts the customer's morale & imagination.

- Letting the family take a look, a shark salesman would have then avoided single biases, since now the entire family is involved in the decision making.

Another example can be from Insurance sector,

If you are selling an insurance product, it is important to understand the customer's requirement for insurance, i.e. insurance amount based on his health, age, family, household income etc.

Involving the customer's wife or husband is critical since the buying decision would impact the entire family as a whole and it is seen that insurance product is never a sole decision.

It is always influenced by the family members.

Points to remember

- Always explore and identify who the true decision maker is for your prospect.
- Ask deep dive questions to understand the prospects emotions, interests and motives.
- Neglect the single biases by involving more decision makers into the process.

Chapter 8

Showing up – A sales virtue.

Sales is a thankless job when it comes to the corporate ecosystem.

Despite of being the revenue generator for the business, the sales team is often looked down upon by other departments.

Internal corporate politics adds further oil to this tension.

So how does a shark salesman tackle internal corporate dynamics?

The answer is in the quote,

"Success is not measured by how high we go up in life, but how many times we bounce back after we fall down."

Resilience & the habit of showing up are the virtues of shark salesman.

In sales there are more rejections i.e. NO's rather than Yes's.

Hence many people call Sales as a business of rejections.

To a normal salesperson, the rejection becomes stressful and demotivating because many tend to take it to their hearts. They started coding their subconscious mind negatively with rejection thoughts.

One failure leads to more failures and the salesman starts losing the self-esteem and start blaming others for his performance.

In my sales career, I have faced more rejections and then successes. The only thing that kept me going is the power of showing up every day at work and making a new start every day.

Being a cricketer in my younger days, the below quote has been itched into my mind.

"You are only as good as your last game".

The shark salesman has to be resilient and keep pushing them despite all the odds.

I happened to watch one of the interviews of the great cricket Sachin Tendulkar, wherein he discloses his secret to success.

"Sweating 10-12 hours daily on the practice nets, irrespective of the tournament or not" .

The single dedication and discipline towards Self-improvement and improving oneself every day, improving averages per game were some of the key secrets of the legendary Sachin Tendulkar.

The shark salesman understands the law of averages in the sales conversion ratio

The sales occurs if the customer finds more benefits towards the solution you are selling and feels less risk in pursuing with your solution.

Lessen the risk or higher the benefits, the more chances for you to close the sale.

Take away point

Lessen the risk for your customer for closing the sale. Put yourself in the customer's shoes.

Build your self esteem

One of the easiest ways to build your self-esteem is by being true to yourself i.e. Be You. Be Honest.

Trying to act like someone else or doing things you hate to do will not help you in the long run.

Use the rejections as a steppingstone and move towards your goals with a razor sharped focus.

Make use of the Paper clip strategy to get back your focus and use the power of visualization for your subconscious mind.

With the same product and under the same circumstances, there are some people who break records while others break themselves.

Build Mental toughness

No two days are same in the sales profession.

There are many days wherein you will face rejections and will feel demotivated.

Building mental toughness will keep you productive. You need to code your mind to read " No" as "Next opportunity" and will keep you moving towards your goals.

The sign of a good shark salesman is that irrespective of the day and circumstances their performance remains consistent.

A boxer, despite being knocked down, gathers courage and strength to rise up and get back to the fight.

Build your GRIT, despite failure you need to show up and continue fighting.

Shark salesman is like a warrior who never gives up.

Build your confidence quotient.

Having a pleasant personality radiating the confidence will open more doors for a good salesman.

<table>
<tr><td>

Point takeaway

People buy confidence and not the product or service.

</td></tr>
</table>

The shark salesman uses self-confidence makes the buyer feel that the seller has something important to say.

A sales professional who radiates confidence is more likely to get an uninterrupted and undivided attention and respect.

Thin line between Persistence and Nagging.

No customer would like to be nagged continuously by the salesman.

However, staying consistently in touch and keep following up are the virtues of a good salesman.

A shark salesman, understand this fact.

He understands that 80% of the sales comes only after 5th follow up. (a research proven fact), however he exercises persistence by not pushing his product or services but by becoming a " Go to" advisor or consultant to his customers.

The best thing in sales in NOT TO SELL.

Become a thought leader & build relationship with your customers so that when they are ready for making the purchase, the only person they think about is YOU.

Everyone wants to win the selling game, but very few are willing to pay the price to prepare to win.

Be punctual

Punctuality is one of the old-fashioned virtues. It costs nothing to be punctual.

Some buyers do test the salesman based on their punctuality.

In my experience while running an advertising firm, I had a customer, who used to organize meeting at 8am or sometimes even at 9pm (night).

On one such instances, he told me the reason for him keeping meetings at odd hours.

The reason which he gave astonished me and gave me my biggest learning.

He said, by keeping the meetings at odd hours, he gets an opportunity to check if he is giving the project to the right people who are committed.

He tested the following virtues of a salesman

- Commitment towards the project
- Punctuality i.e. he can expect the project to be delivered most of the times.
- Assigning the work to the right person who will ensure the project completion.

Point takeaway

Be Punctual, It could be worth more than you think.

You never know who might be testing you and your work.

Chapter 9

Giving up your Ego and Get into your customer mindset.

In my two decades of work experience, one thing that I have learnt in sales profession is that you need to leave your ego at home, before you step out of your home for a sales call.

Do your homework

Once you have established a connection with your prospect and got an appointment; do your research on social media about the person you are going to meet.

His past experiences, common connections and his achievements etc.

May be a common connection or friend can act as a conversation starter with your new prospect or even common interest can prove to be a good conversation starter and create a level of comfort between you and your prospect customer.

There are two types of personality styles.

    a) Thinkers
    b) Feelers.

Thinkers are the people who takes decisions based on numbers, research findings etc whereas the Feelers are the people who are guided by their emotions.

Point takeaway

Logic opens the mind but emotions win the businesses.

Hence I have been always professing the creation of your own tribe and building up of your personal brand.

A shark salesman, understand the buying motive of his customers.

For example, when I used to sell perfumes, I used to understand the customer's expectations from the perfume. Is he looking for functional perfume or is he looking for something that is personal, exclusive and designer to boost his confidence.

I always used to check whether he is looking for daily wear fragrance or for something exclusive for special evening events.

Understanding your prospect's buying motive is very crucial.

Use storytelling

A shark salesman uses stories and analogies to reinforce the sales and make their point.

This reinforces emotional security to the customer.

Statement like:

"We are into the business of crafting memories with our fragrances for over 50 years" reinforces the trust amongst the customers.

'We are the Rolls Royce of fashion".

Ask Questions for deep diving.

There is a saying, "Judge a man not from his looks but by the quality of questions he asks".

A shark salesman's key selling virtue is, asking good questions.

Asking questions and listening carefully helps identifying the latent needs of the prospects.

By asking right questions, you offer choices to the customers to buy what you want to sell him rather than what he intends to buy.

By offering choices, you psychologically motivate the customer to decide which one to buy and move him away from the decision whether to buy or not.

A caution needs to be practiced here i.e. offering too many choices may result in no-sales as well. Hence one need to practice his own judgement.

People buy emotionally.

During one of my holidays, wherein I visited Jaipur and was seeing one of the palaces there. I saw a photography shop which offered a free cold drink to all the tourists entering the palace.

While offering the cold drinks to me and my family, he requested that we try wearing the traditional royal dresses and pose for the picture or memorabilia (memento) with no strings of purchase attached i.e. we would pay for the picture only if we like it.

The deal sounded nice, and we ended up posing like royals and purchasing the picture as well.

Post the trip, I realized that the shop keeper had used the power of Freemium ie. By offering free cold drinks and welcoming us, we felt obligated to return the favor by purchasing the picture.

A very good sales tactic which does not cost you a million of dollars and generate results.

A shark salesman understands the difference between Price and Value.

The most common excuse that a salesman give is of Price, competition is offering lesser prices and discounts.

A shark salesman converts this excuse to his advantage by offering Value, value in terms of educating the customer on the advantages of his product versus competitors.

Playing hard on the emotions i.e. consider buying a product which in long run may prove to be harmful for you versus buying something which will have a healing property in addition to all the deliverables that competiting product is offering.

Play on Value proposition and not on Price.

Using of Verbs for closing a sale.

Verbs like Wow, amazing, awesome sometimes will lead to closing of the sale.

For example a sales man at fashion store, may compliment the customer who tries a particular dress,

"This dress looks amazing, you only need to decide whether you would want to wear it for your special event or for an outing with your friends"

By saying positive comments, you have taken the discussion from whether to buy the dress towards when should I wear this dress as I look stunning in it.

A shark salesman knows the art of closing the sales by offering delight to his/her customers.

Be willing to get into action

During one of my sales visits to one of shops in Bahrain, I observed a customer buying the agarwood and my sales team member was trying to do his best in convincing the customer.

Customer was insisting on the price per 12 gms (agarwood incense is sold in 12gms /tolas)

Before the salesman reveals the price of the agarwood, I jumped into the conversation and took over from my teammate.

I asked the customer; how does it perceive our quality of agarwood and its aroma. The customer replied in affirmative that it is of good quality.

I asked him, to play a game "Guess the price" and tell me a figure that comes to his mind post evaluating our agarwood versus our competition.

He quoted a price which was much higher than our retailing price.

When I revealed our retail selling price, he was delighted and surprised at the same moment.

Surprised to get the real value of his money and delighted to buy a good quality product.

It taught be my biggest lesson in sales

1) Never reveal the price first instead emphasize on the Value that you bring onto the table.

2) Use an idea that can impress and enhance the strength of a sales pitch.

Chapter 10

Visual speaks a thousand words

Every salesman know the fact that visuals speak 1000 words yet only few of them use visuals in their business pitch or sales pitch.

Visual aids (everything from graph or statistics) have to be used in the right way.

Steve job which doing the new launch events used this tool effectively. He used to show the image and used to take a pause and then he used to reveal the relevance of the picture in the new Apple's product.

Apple's famous advertisement – Think Different, is the evidence of this fact.

It showcases the people who thought differently and created a dent in the world with their vision and actions.

Why should we use visuals in our sales pitch?

We live in a time of information overload.

Today, each of us individually generates more information than ever before.

But although the world around us has so rapidly evolved, our brains didn't get a chance to catch up.

The result? Staying focused can quickly become overwhelming.

In a recent survey conducted by Prezi, four out of five professionals admitted that, in the most recent presentation they attended, their attention shifted away from the speaker.

This statistic may come as a shock. But you know what I find the most mind-boggling?

Story telling:

Shark salesmen understand the importance of visual storytelling in the sales process. People think from the heart rather than mind hence it is important to persuade them by influencing their hearts.

If you recall the video done by Dove brand couple of years back called "Real sketches of beauty"

You can check this video on YouTube.

The ad shows women describing themselves to FBI trained forensic artist Gil Zamora (from behind a curtain), who draws a portrait of them based on their description.

Afterwards, a random stranger is asked to describe the same woman to Gil to see how their descriptions would differ.

What we get are two completely different portraits.

The one based on the stranger's portrayal is more beautiful, happier and more accurate.

When Dove reached out to Ogilvy Brazil, the creative agency behind the video, they gave them a straightforward brief: Make women feel better about themselves.

They knew the statistics. Only 4% of women around the globe feel good about themselves. The idea was to prove them wrong about their self-image.

With the concept of "Real Beauty Sketches," they assumed that women would probably describe themselves in a more negative way than perceived by a stranger.

Visual tools are of utmost importance if you want to stimulate your prospect's imagination and persuade him to think about your product or services more from the heart.

Visuals help in establishing " Dil ka rista" (urdu words which means enticing & wining your prospects heart).

I used this technique during my sales pitch with my customers while selling luxury niche fragrances.

I used to carry the entire collection (7 fragrances) in a kit which carried an iPad.

Firstly, I used to show the video explaining the concept of the fragrances and why the concept is unique and very niche and post evoking the prospect's imagination, I used to let them go try their hands on all the fragrances wherein they used to appreciate the fragrance notes, the concept or theme behind the creation of the fragrances.

The end result – I always used to leave my prospects mesmerized in their imagination which appealed to them more than presenting any statistics or boring sales pitches. They lingered the fragrances for hours and it helped me a salesperson to stay on top of their mind & close the sales.

Can visual storytelling be used in other industrial goods?

Yes it can be used in industrial selling as well. For example consider yourself a salesman selling mining drill equipment.

Due to large size of the equipment, it is next to impossible to give onsite demo of the drill machine, instead you could carry a piece of granite, narrating the story of the history and formation of the granite rock (i.e. how many years old and how strong rock is granite) and show a piece of the granite rock which is cut into pieces by the drilling machine, the surface of the granite cut as smooth as a butter itself.

This communicates the robustness of your drill machine alongside excites the imagination of your prospect to give your drilling equipment a try.

Ikea, the Swedish retailer, uses visual storytelling to the core.

They create the demo homes inside their stores featuring their furniture, which makes their customer imagine their furniture in their homes and how good would it look into their homes.

Shark salesman uses the power of persuasion using the visual tools or aids to their advantages.

Use visuals even when you are selling boring accounting services, you can create interesting graphs and infographics to show how your accounting services has helped your clients to increase their profits i.e. through cash flow management, better account receivables etc.

Building recall

The ability the customer will have of recalling the information 3 hours after you present is 3x higher when presenting verbally and visually than if you just talk to them.

And even more incredibly, the ability of the potential customer to recall information 3 days after the presentation increases 7x when both visual and verbal are used in a presentation!

Point takeaway

- Use visual story telling in your sales pitches
- Increases engagement
- Persuasive selling
- Increases Brand Recall.

Chapter 11

Prospecting and Conversation starters.

Prospecting is lifeblood and key to success in sales.

Prospective is more than a skill, I would like to call it an attitude, a habit.

A shark salesman is always on the lookout for prospecting options, while visiting a client's office in the business district, he scans the prospects while scanning the companies available in that district and who may be interested in the products or services that the salesman offers.

Prospecting is a continuous process and in the age of social commerce and social media it has become an important tool to reach your prospect's mind directly.

Who is prospect?

Your customer becomes prospect, when he has

- The money to buy your product or service
- Intent clarity to buy

- Facing issues which your product can solve.
- Someone in the decision making capacity.

A shark salesman creates a big pipeline of prospects and works on the multiple approaches to build this pipeline of prospective customers. Few of them are mentioned below.

- Networking – either in personal or on social media networks.
- Industry association memberships.
- Referrals from partners and existing clients
- Creating their inbound funnels and producing industry relevant content
- Cold calling – though many think its outdated but still very relevant
- Personal branding on social media- projecting thought leadership.

In previous chapter, I have described of Paper clip strategy, it is an important tool for prospecting customers through cold calls, direct emails , newsletters etc.

Any prospecting method requires a fuel called "Follow up".

Prospecting fails if they are not pursued or followed up regularly. Average thumb rule states that customer tends to become ready to at least meet you and hear your proposal is after 4 follow-ups.

Converting the meeting with the prospect into sales needs a series of follow-ups and different techniques for building trust with the prospect and becoming a "Go To advisor" from a mere salesperson.

Many of us participate in trade events and exhibitions wherein we collect the business cards from the prospects who come to our booth to check out our product or services.

But do you know, how many of them actually do a follow up, as per a study just 20% people share the generic thank you mail and only 7% sends a couple of follow up emails.

Hence the impact of participating in an exhibition is lost.

The game of follow-ups and putting all the business leads in to sales funnel starts post exhibitions.

- It starts with sending a thank you note.
- Followed up by email addressing a specific enquiry raised by the prospect during the visit
- Followed up by a call to understand how crucial is the solution for the prospect.
- Deep diving into the prospect's actual issue
- Preparing a proposal
- Removing the Buyer's risk from the proposal
- Meeting the customer for the final pitch.
- Closing of the sale.

(This process may vary from industry to industry but the premise of the context remains same).

Existing customers are the best source of referrals.

Ask all your customers to refer you to their counterparts within their sector or send e-introduction mail to their counterparts, introducing you and your company.

Testimonials generation from your happy customers goes a long way in building trust amongst your prospects.

Always put a video testimonials on your website and social media pages.

Conversation starters

Once you are ready with the prospect list. Now you need to approach them & introduce yourself and your product as quickly as possible.

Introduction is the ice breaker for any conversation.

I shall share a hack here which I learnt from the book by the author Simon Tupman –"why entrepreneurs should eat bananas"

He narrated a concept of "spoken logo" in his book

The concept include "your key work & perceived benefit' in your introduction.

Instead of saying – I am an Accountant,

You say, " I help my clients by taking away hassles and time to maintain their books and records up to date, so that they could well spend their time in growing business."

In case you are a legal advisor, you could say, " I help my clients with my bespoke legal contracts which protect their interests in any acquisitions or mergers".

Personally, I use the following in my introduction being a retail expert.

"I help retailers to come out of the valley of death by handholding them in their retail journey and helping them to scale their retail business".

"Spoken Logo" is a very powerful hack, and it builds immediate connection with your prospect.

Few text books suggest the following rules to be followed while starting conversations with your prospects.

- Your opening sentence must grab the prospect's attention.
- Get to the point immediately
- Your opening statement must include a benefit statement.
- Always put yourself in the receiver's position and develop your intro accordingly.

A shark salesman listens to his prospects views and ask the questions to deep dive into the issues that are being faced by the prospects.

Basically, their conversation starters converts the cold leads into warm leads and finally into HOT leads.

A shark salesman work on 80% of the hot leads in order to deliver & achieve sales targets while staying in contact with the cold and warm prospects and work on converting them to HOT leads.

Point takeaway

- Prepare your introduction well in advance as you may not know when you may have to use.
- Follow up is the fuel for any prospecting.

Use Comm- YOU-nicaton

Using "You" first gets much better response. In his book "How to talk to anyone" author leil lowndnes explain this concept.

For instance, when you ask to your manager for a leave, which of the following option do you think will get you positive result.

"sir can I get a leave coming Friday?"

Or

"Sir, can you do without me on Friday?"

The first question will provoking the manager to think, "Can I let go this person for a day" this is an additional work for the decision maker.

In the second option, Your wording made managing without you a matter of pride for Boss.

"Of course I can manage with you" is what comes to your manager's mind immediately as his instant response.

Hence the second worded question will have a better chance of getting a positive reply.

This technique is called "Comm-YOU-nication"

By putting YOU in the sentence, you have pre-guided the response that you wanted from your manager.

A shark salesman uses this technique to their advantage.

A good salesman by putting or using YOU in his communication evokes positive responses from their customers.

"I like the your dress" versus " YOU look great in that dress" which one do you think will evoke warmer response from your customer.

If you say, the second one, then you have understood this concept.

Start using YOU in your communications as it grabs your listener's attention. It gets you positive response most of the times.

Chapter 12

Right sales attitude.

Selling is nothing but the transfer of right enthusiasm from the seller to the buyer.

Right sales attitude is the core attribute to become a good shark salesman.

a) Having a strong conviction about the product or service you are selling

While selling a luxury brand of fragrance, one customer asked me which is your favorite fragrance and why.

I replied to him handing over one of my favorite and the most expensive fragrance to him and I told him this is one of my favorite fragrances not just because it carries spicy notes which uplifts my spirits but since it is one of the most exclusive fragrance and only selected few like and buy it.

"It's one of the most niche fragrance available in the region. Would you like to try it?"

This statement arouse curiosity of my customer and he sprayed the fragrance twice on him and agreed with me on the story which I had narrated him.

He Infact ended up purchasing a USD 800 worth of that fragrance bottle.

Point to remember

Selling is 90% conviction and 10% communication of the conviction.

To develop right attitude in sales you must do the following

- Unbiased self-control and focus on your goals, for which you have to write your goals.
- 100% commitment to self-education and development
- Always ready to give and help
- Listening to your customers
- Lead generation and prospecting
- Learning to build trust amongst their team mates and customers.
- Overcoming resistance from the customers by asking relevant questions
- Providing solutions
- Build post purchase rapport, this can be done by asking the customer to like your FB page or adding them to LinkedIn page of the company and staying connected with them.

I strongly believe that salesman are made and not born. With right skills and attitude one can become a shark salesman.

Never give up attitude:-

Most salesman, approaches a customer through cold calling and if they are lucky, they send their proposal to the customer and follows up after a day or two.

Upon hearing or getting a negative reply, they stop chasing the prospect.

Whereas a shark salesman, upon hearing the negative reply, puts the customer on the medium hot lead section on his excel sheet and adds the prospect to mailing list for getting informative articles on the product or the sector- what's happening in the world of business etc.

He develops a channel of communication with the prospect by means of mailers or personalized mails.

When he feels that the prospect is ready to purchase, they come with a proposal which good enough not to be refused.

Money lies in follow-ups and building trust and your re-targeting strategies.

In a study it was found out that the business gets closed in the seventh follow up when selling high ticket items.

How many of you currently do follow ups 7 times? Answer would be very few.

This is what differentiates between a good salesman versus average salesman.

3A's of shark salesman:

Attitude – which is never give up or stand up even if you fail in closing the sale.

Ambition – aspiration to achieve your set goals, tasks.

Action – Putting strategies into action which takes you closer to your goals and close your sales.

There is no shortcut to develop strong mental attitude, you have code your mind consistently with positive quotes, affirmations that you will succeed and there is no better salesmen than you.

You are UNIQUE and offer the best service to your customers.

Self-discipline

Self-discipline forms a habit amongst a shark salesman.

They code their mind only with positive affirmations and do the tasks even if they hate to do it.

If it got to be done, shark salesman just jumps and do the task even if they hate it.

That's called the self-discipline.

(if you have to make 20 sales calls, then they make 20 calls even if they don't like doing it. They would also attend networking events to keep their pipeline of orders active and growing).

Self-check: No pain No gain.

Most of the selling process requires writing proposal based on a customer's needs.

Every customer is unique with unique problems to solve.

Most salespeople tend to avoid writing the proposal and tend to take refuge to cut & paste from their previous proposal.

This is completely a wrong practice, every proposal need to be rewritten, redrafted keeping in mind the customer's requirements and as to how your business shall add value to your clients.

A clear value or benefit proposition is a must to be communicated along with set clear deliverables.

Reading your proposal, the customer should feel that his pain point is being addressed promptly.

My advice to shark salesman is to read the proposal at least 2-3 times prior to sending it to your customer.

Avoid spelling and grammatical errors, get it vetted by a third party in case you are sending a technical proposal.

During my tenure with a digital agency, I had made this mistake of forwarding the creative artwork to the client without checking the copy text matter.

The copy text matter had some spell errors which was pointed out by the customer and later corrected by us, and it was quite embarrassing for me and took lot of corrective actions to amend the relationship with the client.

So, rechecking the proposal is always a good exercise and Standard operating procedure.

Chapter 13

Minimize your customer's risk.

In any sales negotiations, as a good salesman, you need to evaluate the pros & cons of the discussion that you are going to undertake with your customer.

Understanding the parameters that influence his decision are key to winning & closing the sales.

Eliminating the risk or minimizing the risk that your customer may perceive is the best way to close the sales.

During your meeting with the prospect, ask many questions that may lead you to the parameters that are going to be crucial in closing the deal with your customer.

Many buyers sometimes feel driven by fear of unknown and take time to decide. Their fear could be due to lack of knowledge, lack of experience, what will my boss or board of director say or react to my decision.

They tend to worry about consequences if the product does not work or perform as expected.

These fears or concerns may hamper your prospects of closing the sale with that particular customer.

The best policy is to address all these fears and mitigate them even before you start highlighting about your product or solution's USPs.

In case you are running your ecommerce business, you can offer free returns or money back guarantee in case your product does not meets your customer's expectation.

Offering money back or free returns option on your ecommerce site help you to build TRUST with your customers and helps you to improve your click through rate (CTR) that means your customer acquisition cost goes down with period.

Offering Buy Now Pay later (BNPL) options on your site also improves customer's experience since by providing them monthly installments plan, you are mitigating their risk of paying a lumpsum in advance for your product.

In physical retail, one of the electronic retailers that I had worked previously offered "Money Back guarantee" in case your favorite gadget is not in the store.

A well-known electronic retailer in the UAE had made a promise to its customers, "in case we don't carry that particular model of the gadget, we shall get it for you in 48 hours, otherwise we will pay for the product".

This single promise built the brand in the middle east as they promised to carry large varieties and large brand mix to their customers.

Travel site MakeMyTrip also had similar promise when they started, their promise stated, "If you find the ticket cheaper anywhere, we will pay you the difference back".

This mitigates the risk of purchasing of air tickets at lowest cost and builds trust amongst the customers.

Tip to remember

- Always seek ways to mitigate or reduce risk for your customers.

Commercially, such tactics work well in practice as the main aim of any business is to acquire customers and retain them by making them used to your product or services.

Initially you pay more to acquire customers but over a period the acquisition cost comes down and that is the concept of Lifetime Value of the customer. (LTV).

In insurance selling business, the most companies, pay the installment for their customers in order to acquire them. It is seen that in insurance business model, the customer tends to stay with the insurance for longer duration i.e. 10 years or so or till the policy maturity yield is completed.

Hence you would have noticed that your first month premium is normally paid by the insurance company as a marketing cost to acquire you as a customer.

During my tenure with perfumery, I was tasked with development of Private label manufacturing. I had engaged in discussion with one of the prospects who wanted to develop their own range of fragrances and were looking for vendors who could everything for them right from conceptualization to product designing, product packaging's, perfume selection and finally the final product.

Post 2-3 meetings with them they had shortlisted our company but were not closing the order. I thought this could be due to their inherent fear.

I invited them to visit our production facilities and took their trip to our head office and factory as an opportunity to showcase both our production strength as well as our brand building capabilities of over 50 years in the market place.

By mitigating their fear, I was able to close the deal and build a stronger bond with them.

> Having a satisfied and happy customer is the best business strategy ever.

Chapter 14

Speak your customer language & entice them with your words.

Empathy is the ability to put ourselves mentally in the other person's shoes & is essential for success, especially in Sales.

Sales persons must be sensitive to the reactions of their customers.

Dale Carnegie's gave two principles for practicing Empathy

"Become genuinely interested in the other person."

"Try honestly to see things from the other person's point of view".

Another sales technique is called "Parroting" which is explained below.

If you are selling electrical appliances and your customer comes to your shop in a hot humid weather and says, "its too hot today".

As a good salesman, you need to acknowledge his comment in affirmative, " Yes you are right, its too hot and humid", " why don't you come inside and relax and let me show you some our large varieties of electrical fans which can help you cool and relax"

Immediate acknowledging the customer's feedback, you are creating a sense of comfort for the customer and he feels relaxed that you will understand his pain points or requirements.

Parroting or echoing is a simple linguistic technique which creates a subliminal rapport with your customers.

It makes them feel you share their values, their attitudes, their interests, their experiences.

In case of global business, wherein you have customers across different continents and speak different languages, as a good shark salesman, you need to show

- Stress on Nonverbal communication
- Try to break the barrier by using and learning some important words from your customer's region. Mainly greetings words, salutation words etc.

Salutation works wonder in sales. I learnt the same while handling one of the Japanese brand called Sanrio, which is famous for their merchandise Hello Kitty.

My immediate manager had told me to use a salutation called "San" post saying the name of any Japanese person, to show the respect.

It really helped my working with our brand owners when communicating with them either verbal or written communication.

My tenure of working in Indian market, taught me this aspect of speaking or greeting your customers in their language added value in all my workings especially with our stockists and distributors and helped me win their trust.

My Indian market exposure in sales and distribution taught me a greatest lesson,

You can resolve any business issues with your stockists by greeting him- "namaste Bhai Saheb"

These two words can make a stranger your closest allies in the market place.

In India, you win friends over a cup of chai (tea) and using words like "Bhai", "Bhai Saheb" etc.

I loved every moment of my market visits across the country, whether Kerala, Karnataka, Tamil nadu , Gujrat , Punjab.

These small learnings really helped me develop my network with my stockists and dealers. Of course, you need to action your words by helping or resolving stockists key issues, which were according to me were mainly - processing of their claims, given out during the promotions.

India as a country is very unique, wherein friendship bonds are created over a cup of hot chai and by using words which entice your customer to start trusting you and once that bond is formed, you can move mountains in the marketplace.

In FMCG business, you are only as strong as your network of dealers and distributors. If your sales team lacks this bond with their supply chain members, you are going to face tough competition from your internal customers, not to mention your competitors in the market place.

Chapter 15

Sales training.

"The greatest crime in the world is not developing your potential. When you do what you do best, you are helping not only yourself, but the world." Roger Williams.

This quote is so very relevant when it comes to building a sales team and training them to believe your brand's purpose and vision.

No matter how competent we may be, unless we can sell our ideas to others we may fall short of success.

Whether it is persuading senior management of your company to implement some suggestions you have made or pushing your sales team members to sell more.

If we sincerely believe in what we are selling, it is not difficult to project that to others.

One of the key factors that can either break you or make you is your -strong commitment for continuous improvement.

That's where continuous training programs and sales events comes into the picture.

Most of the sales people in an organization sees the training event as a paid holiday, involving 5 star hotel's lunches or dinners;

Post the training event 95% of the participants forget as to what they had learnt or taught and they get back to their standard work profile.

Few tips for the trainers to make their training content more memorable.

Keep the customer in mind always

- Look for the issues that the customer is facing with the organization, it may be internal customer or external customer.
- List some of the core issues in the training material.

Challenge the sales team

Ask them to come prepared with well thought out solutions to these issues from their own perspectives.

- Present a clear, reasonable vision of the "should be" situation.
- Create realistic timetables. (Post training)
- Create learning and development plans online which a sales team has to undergo consistently to learn and upgrade themselves.
- The scores of the training tests should form the basis of their sales performance appraisals.

Creation of L&D (learning & development) budget

Most companies, want the best of the salesman but very few are ready to commit themselves on the path of developing their sales teams on consistent basis.

Making major changes, like every aspect of business, costs money.

Budget allocation in training and communicating the brand's vision and strategy to the sales team need to be informed on regular periods.

Prepare a change-management plan wherein you communicate the aspirations of the management and define a road map and show a clear path to your sales team.

"Planning is the open road to your destination. If you don't know where you are going, how do you expect to get there?"

– Basil Walsh.

Dynamics of a learning sales organizations.

a) Build a core team of senior managers who would act as a mentor to the sales team and will help them in their issues by showing them the correct path.

b) Involve the key stakeholders in the process who would mentor the group and act as a "guide".

Informal leaders are often loaded with ideas and suggestions on how to make things better.

c) Communicate Vision.

Vision and mission statement are not only plaques which are hung on the walls of the business offices or at receptions.

They are the core values which everyone right from the business owner to the lowest ranks of the organization should embody and live it every day and every moment.

d) Feedback loop

Leaders create feedback loop to improvise on their strategy, so listening here becomes the true virtue. Involve your sales team to come up with out of the box solutions to outperform competition in the marketplace.

e) Create cross functional teams

One thing which sets Amazon.com apart from its competitors is the team creation.

They create small teams for every project they undertake, whether it is creation of AWS or Prime or Alexa voice enabled searches.

The cross functional teams work as a business unit and are responsible for the project completion and deliverables. They are

empowered to take risks and innovate. They are
not pulled up for failures in innovating.

Their main purpose is to keep innovating.

Champions never say, "It can't be done". They
try to find a way to overcome the hurdles. Even
champions don't always win, but they always
learn from their failures and improvise on it.

f) Training is an ongoing endeavor.
Methodologies like "train the trainer" and then
let the trainer train his team is one of such
practices applied in the sales training.

We all are selling continuously, selling to our managers, to
our customers, selling to our teammates. Selling is
essential to success.

The first step in sales is to be well prepared .
Comprehensive knowledge on your services or product,
market place, why your offer is the best or unique, what
make your brand stand out from the clutter.

Sales trainings – Must include

- Selling Strategies.
- All the training should be focused on developing
  sales team on selling skills, it should include the

soft skills as well as tricks & hacks which can lead to immediate sales increase.

- Product Knowledge – this is core function of the sales training.
- Buyer Persona- How to Create customer's persona or segmentation and train salesman on the strategies to deal with each persona and strategies needed.
- Competitor Analysis – Most of the sales organization provide the formats to collect the competitors data or intelligence. Structured data reporting on market intelligence helps in decision making.
- Time Management – The most crucial aspect as to how much time a salesman need to spend on his/her sales call. Creation of customer's persona comes to help in managing your time per customer. Incase the customer is always nagging but buys in bulk, it makes more sense to spend more time with that customer and mitigate all his issues and fears.
- Sales Forecast – The biggest hindrance for any sales organization is to forecast the sales trend for next year or 3 years horizon. Training events should be conducted for teaching the sales team to gather the correct data, corelate them so that they make sense and forecast the previous sales periods with the projected months in line with management's directives.

I shall dedicate a chapter on creation of Buyer's persona later in the book.

Chapter 16

Price as a selling tool.

Customers love bargaining.

Actually, everyone love negotiating on the prices.

How many sites do we browse to find lower air ticket? The answer would be approx. 5-6 sites.

All we look is lower fares.

Question is how a shark salesman utilize this behaviour of seeking discounts or bargain to his advantage.

Price is always a sensitive issue in selling.

Having faced numerous customers during my career in beauty industry, let me narrate you an anecdote when I was responsible for selling an ultra niche perfume brand, the average price of our fragrances were in the range of USD 1500 and above.

During my sales visit to one of our stores, I met a customer who showed a keen interest in our fragrances and had narrowed down his selection to the oud fragrance (agarwood incense which has oriental flavours), the cost of the fragrance was around USD 1800/-

Customer : It's too expensive fragrance. Way out of my budget.

Me: Yes you are right sir, its expensive.

But allow me to explain the reason, the fragrance which are holding in your hand comes from one of the rarest agarwood tree, aged for over 25 years and is bottled in to glass bottle which hand blown Murano glass.

Moreover, the blend gives the lasting longevity to the fragrance for over 24 hours.

My reply was the last thing the customer had expected i.e. I acknowledge the fact that our fragrances were ultra-luxury niche fragrances.

But he got convinced when he heard the emotive benefits that were associated with the product.

In other words, the price is described as high if the product were much less valuable than it is, but as necessary, understandable, for what the product benefits actually delivers.

In the above example, I used the technique which I had explaining in my previous chapter called Parroting or Echoing and supported with the emotive product benefit pitch that the price tag looked smaller.

This technique not only work, it also surprises and customers concentrate at once when you agree with something that they had expected would start an argument or whole bargaining process.

Another way to address the price question is to separate the "Price" from the overall buying process.

Creative shark salesman use a technique called – story telling using Metaphor.

Dale cargenie advice fits.

"The only way on earth to influence people is talk about what they want, and show them how to get it."

The trick is removing the price from the selling equation completely using story telling format.

An excellent example is Apple Inc.

If you recall, they had initially used a communication "Think differently" . the ad showed the pictures of great visionaries like Nelson Mandela, Mahatma Gandhi, wright brothers etc.

The advertisement was an excellent example of Persuasive selling.

It showed the customers that brand stood for "challenging the norms"

It showed personality who thought differently in order to make the world a better place and created history.

People related to the Apple's vision and persuasive communication, and we know the rest is History.

How to overcome price objections in B2B sector?

The scenario differs when you are selling tech goods or services to businesses.

Always ask your customer,

"expensive in compared to…" ,

often the customer has their pre-notions about the product and services and upon hearing those concerns, as a shark salesman you need to address their issues and resolve.

Use persuasive words.

> "Let's say money was no object. Would our product/service help solve your problem?"

If the customer responds in positive that he likes the product or service, then you as a salesman need to work out a payment plan which covers both the customer's price objection and your company's interest.

> "Will price keep you from getting what you really want?"

By using this statement, you try to answer the pros of the deal and cons for not choosing your product or services.

Use snowballing question affect.

Does this mean we will never have the chance to work together?"

When it comes to handling sales objections, '**never**' is the most powerful word in the English language,

"Most people hate it. As a result, the vast majority of prospects will respond by saying, 'well, no … not *never*!'"

This gives you an option to ask your customer to list all his concerns and try to address them wherever you can.

The most common customer's reply,

"I will come back to you later as I need to think your proposal through"

Most of the indecisive customers say this line and a well-trained shark salesman should immediately acknowledge the customer sentence by

"Which part of the proposal you want to think over?

Is there something about our creditably or Is it the investment?

Listen to customer replies carefully in case he answers NO to your questions means he does not have any issues pertaining your proposal.

The moment you hear any hidden objection whether it is "Price" or "post sales service" you need to immediately address these concerns and fears and resolve.

Chapter 17

Best way to sell is Not to sell

Listening is a virtue and most salesman lacks the same.

They need to be trained and learn the art of listening by asking the right questions.

Questions engage the customer into a dialogue and the shark salesman uses this technique to listen to the customer's responses to alter or adapt his selling pitch.

Sales is a two way dialogue between the seller and the buyer.

The shark salesman, would immediately seek permission of the customer to ask questions,

"Sir, in order to serve you better, would you allow me to ask some questions to understand your requirements correctly"

Seeking permission to ask show humility and respect towards the customer and will be appreciated by the customer.

There are two types of popular questions formats.

- Open ended – which gives the customer to provide explanation or his pain points which he wants to be addressed with the solution or product that you are providing.
- Close ended – these are questions which has replies in YES or NO.

A good salesman will use these two questions formats to discover the customer's actual requirements and would provide solutions accordingly (tailor made solutions in case of B2B selling).

Salesman should consider themselves as a doctor.

If you consult a doctor, you would observe that the doctor firstly makes you comfortable, ask you questions on what your pain points or illness are, check for the symptoms, if required, he would refer some tests to validate his diagnosis.

By asking questions, he determines the source of illness, is it aggravated by consuming wrong food, is it flu or any pre-existed complications.

No matter what you sell, selling principles are fundamental and applied universally across the industries.

A word of caution here.

A good salesman would avoid asking stupid questions like,

"Do you prefer cheaper or cost reduction option?"

Never use words like cheap, or lower costs since they disallow further engagement and challenges the buyer's intelligence.

Always ask questions which makes the customer thinking.

"Can you imagine the turnaround using your own customer database and generating a sales turnaround"?

This question will prompt your customer to think on various possibilities which they would have not even considered, and they will be more open to listen to your solutions and keen to understand your rationale.

Key take outs:

- Ask questions which are open ended and less on close ended.
- Don't sound stupid while questioning
- Always seek permission to ask question, it shows honesty and humility & respect.

Why Ask questions?

- Questions put you in charge of the discussion, you lead the conversation with your customer.
- Helps you uncover the customer's needs
- Helps you identify the decision maker
- Brings out the fear of the customer in making decisions in your favor.
- Encourages a discussion rather than a monologue.

Use deep diving questions to understand the real crux of the problem underlying with the customer's internal operational processes.

"Do you think, it would be fair to ask you to kindly elaborate further what you mentioned just now…"

"What seems to your concern"

Few tricks for salesman to prepare prior to meeting the customer

- Rehearse in your mind as to how would you like to engage the customer into a discussion.
- Find out the key questions that can help you uncover the customer's requirements
- Ask the questions which will help you decide if the customer really need your product or service at the first place.
- Use consultative selling approach – rehearse the questions first which would help you uncover the prospect's needs or pain points.

To explain this further using my own tried and tested formula.

Imagine you are selling perfumes, the customer walks into your store.

Salesman: Good morning, Sir, welcome to the world of fragrances, how may I help you?

Customer: Good morning, I am just checking out?

Salesman: that's great to hear. we carry the largest varieties of oriental fragrances and some of the rarest fragrances found in the oriental world.

(By stating that you show humility as well as have pitched about the USP of your store)

Customer – wow, I would like to explore the fragrances.

Salesman – please allow me to assist you and take you on journey into the mystic world of fragrances and their history. By the way what type of fragrances you prefer the most?

"Do you like evening wear fragrance" or "day long fragrances" or "fragrance for special occasions".

By seeking to find out more about the customer's preferences you can then suggest or show him/her the fragrances that can entice their mood and make them purchase your product.

Show customer the respect even when he decides not to purchase or give you business.

Make sure that you make the customer feel like king for the time he spent in your store. You need to make sure he feels welcomed and honored.

Sell me this Pen

This narrative has become very famous, thanks to the movie of Jordan Belfort, The wolf of wall street.

Customer: sell me this pen

Salesman: sure sir, but please allow me to ask you a question, " why do you need this pen"?

Customer: I need the pen to write my goals and purpose.

Salesman: Sir, that's great objective, but what more do you want to fulfill with this pen?

Customer: it serves and satisfies my aspirations as it is a brand of repute. Helps me make a powerful impression in the meetings.

Salesman: Lovely, how much are you willing to spend for making an impactful presence in your circle of influence?

Customer: anything around USD 350-500

Sales man: sure I would let you have your most powerful tool for USD 350/-.

Just analyze who sold to whom.

Customer sold the pen to himself. That's the way of selling.

"To sell more... don't sell" is the mantra.

Chapter 18

Listening – a selling virtue.

I am a big devotee of lord Ganesh.

One of my learnings from Lord Ganesha; Lord has two big ears and one small mouth.

What that signifies to us as human beings?

"Listen More and talk less."

"Stay so close to your customers that you can understand them completely and make them aware of your services even before they realize that they need your services"

One the key virtue in sales is Listening.

It is universal virtue, but a good salesman knows when he or she has to adapt to this virtue while in the selling process and also to whom they are selling.

If you are speaking to the CEO about some high-priced technical software solution, then

Executives typically expect you to understand their business and challenges before you talk with them.

You build credibility by showing them you are knowledgeable about their business.

Additionally, they expect that you are going to tell them business lessons to be learned from their peers at other companies.

Shark salesmen should ask questions that get the end-users to conclude there is a large gap between their current state and the desired future state.

Discovery is the name of the game.

To do good discovery the salesman needs to actively listen by paraphrasing what s/he heard, clarifying, and using a lot of 'walk me through' or 'tell me more' type phrases.

Mediums to listen to your prospect.

Cold calls - require the seller to establish context and say something of value to earn the right to ask questions.

(inbound leads) follow a different pattern. Your reps should be talking much less, around 35-45% of the time

Prospects who fill out web forms to request a call with a salesman typically are in an active buying cycle.

They have an issue to address, something they need to accomplish, or a risk to mitigate.

As such the job of the salesman changes. In a cold call, context is needed. In these calls the buyer already has context. Now the salesman needs to move right to discovery to get the prospect to open up and talk more.

The salesman has earned the right to ask questions by virtue of the work that marketing has done educating the buyer and either getting them to call a phone number or request a meeting.

discovery calls are all about asking questions, checking understanding, confirming, clarifying, and active listening. They require somewhere around a 60:40 to 75:25 talk to listen ratio.

Prototype demos or live case studies

Showcasing your strengths in terms of producing results is one way to entice your prospect to buy your services.

People buy results.

Be an active listener

Active listening goes beyond listening to include paying close attention, focusing to eliminate distractions and devoting mental effort to process what's being said.

Active listening isn't easy and doesn't come naturally.

When people are actively listening, they respond differently than those who are only partly engaged.

A Shark salesman exhibit the qualities of Active listeners by

- They don't interrupt – they let their customer talk more
- They avoid being judgmental – they don't jump into the conclusions.
- Probe for clarification, back story, details and feelings.
- They try to Listen for both content and feeling.
- Empathize by putting themselves in the speaker's shoes.
- Listen for what's different, not just for what's familiar.
- Take what's being said seriously.
- Take notes or record the conversations so that they are refer to them while preparing the proposals.

In order to improve or learn listening skills, I would recommend reading the Robert Cialdini's book, "The Art of Presuasion".

Listening is very different from Hearing.

Listening is more emotive i.e., emotional, you are taking notes of the changes in the tones and behavior of the prospect when he or she is talking to you.

Active listening will give you the clues and help you identify the buying motives.

Use para phrasing regularly to encourage your prospect to talk more about his requirements and under lying pain points.

"Can you please elaborate a little more…"

"that's sound like a master stroke."

Talk less to sell more:

I learnt this from my CEO of liht organics, Ms. Nerissa Low.

During one of the sales pitch meetings with one of the prospects, she noticed and gave me her candid feedback to improve.

She said, "Ritesh you are a good talker, and your talking helps in closing a sale, but you should know when to stop talking and when to start listening."

This feedback made me think of myself and my selling process and I realized where I was making a mistake and I started working on myself to improve.

Giving too much of the information in the beginning to the prospect may confuse or overwhelm the customer.

A shark salesman needs to learn "how much" is "too much" in terms of content.

Taking notes and post meeting recap & follow up

From my experience, I have noticed that one-third of your sales goes wasted if you don't have follow up mechanisms.

Now with the advent of tech tools, the follow up has become easy.

You could retarget your prospect on social media by showing him the content that helps him remember you.

Your regular newsletters will keep your prospect connected with you as you would provide useful actionable tips in your newsletters and live case studies.

A shark salesman is not only proficient in selling but he acknowledges the fact the sales success is hidden in the "follow ups".

He initiates & develops is own follow up mechanism which may include writing personal short emails , social media connections etc.

<table>
<tr><td>

Key takeaways:

- Money lies in follow ups.
- Be an active listener
- Should know how to reveal in the first meeting.
- Talk less.

</td></tr>
</table>

Chapter 19

Overcoming Rejections.

People often ask me, "Ritesh how come you are so visible on social media?"

Most of you who knows me or are connected with me on social media (LinkedIn, Facebook, Instagram or tiktok) would see me posting educational and informative posts on daily basis.

My answer is all my readers is

"Consistency" beats "Talent" hands down, at any given day.

So how do you measure success?

Success is not measured by how high we go up in life, but how many times we bounce back after we fall down.

Failures & rejections are nothing but a steppingstone to success.

If you are not failing, you are not progressing.

Why am I talking about failures and rejections in my book which is dedicated to sales management?

The answer is simple, "Selling is equivalent to Rejection business".

Ask any sales manager of any company, he would say that they all come across rejections from their prospects regularly and the only thing that keeps them going forward is the love and passion for their profession of sales.

With every rejection, comes pain, stress and more important more sales pressures from your organizational heads.

So, what makes some salesman – super heroes or super salesman?

One of the things that I have seen in super successful sales professionals in my career, they all had a very high self-esteem and self- confidence.

They have taken ownership and accountability towards their profession.

As I pen down this chapter, I recall a scene from a very popular Bollywood movie, "Guru" which was inspired by the life of a very successful Indian entrepreneur, who went on to build his global empire.

One of the famous dialogue which the main protagonist used to say frequently, " I cannot hear No" i.e. he had coded his mind to ignore the answer NO whenever he was shunned away by his prospective customers.

Ignoring or handling rejections made this entrepreneur built his global empire.

Personally, speaking I too have coded my mind to translate "NO" as "Next opportunity". Whenever my proposal or sales pitch gets rejected, I tell these two words to myself and keep on moving forward.

So what do these super salesman do which others are not doing?

The answer to these question, lies in a word " Persistence"

Winners do things in spite of problems and loser tend to give up when they hit the wall.

Key takeaway:

It is with stress; few stones get crushed whereas very few of them turn out to be diamonds".

What is Persistence?

Let me narrate you a story of a man as an example of Persistence and who went through a journey, called **"life"** like a marathon.

Few credentials from his Resume:

- At age of 21, he saw his first business fail.
- When he was 23, he ran for a political office and lost.

- At age of 24, he saw his second business fail
- 29, he again contested for elections and lost
- At 31, he again contested for elections and lost again
- At 37, he contested for elections and finally won.

Looking at these credentials, will anyone from the corporate world hire such a candidate?

My answer is the same as yours i.e. in negative.

The above credentials not only shows persistence but reveals a great deal of patience.

In the end, it paid off – for he was none other than Abraham Lincoln who at the age of 51 became the sixteenth President of the United States of America.

The Only way to build Persistence and Overcome Rejection is to build **Mental toughness.**

> "If your mind can conceive something and your heart can believe it, your body can achieve it".

Always remember…

I would urge all readers of this book, to watch an English Movie "Pursuit of Happiness" and see as to what persistence is and hard work that the main protagonist undergoes & overcomes it with his professional attitude and then success embraces him.

The movie is based on true life story of Chris Gardener, a successful businessman.

Introspection of the rejection or Postmortem of Rejection

Every rejection needs to be introspected, evaluated with facts and narrated as to why the deal or proposal could not go through

- Was it the customer, not ready to buy now (then that leads should be parked in cold lead which could be converted into hot lead in future)
- Was the proposal too complicated for easy understanding?

All the aspects of the sales process need to be evaluated and action plan needs to be devised to overcome these short falls in the future.

Basically, learning how to get better at getting better – is the mantra for success in Sales.

Chapter 20

ABC principle of selling.

"Always be closing" is what ABC principle of selling means.

The sales is not complete till the prospect buys your product or service and pays for it.

A sales closing is an art of selling and most importantly the way of presenting to your customers.

If you have a made a good sales pitch or good presentation, you have almost nailed down the selling process.

When I was handling a departmental store Woolworths in the middle east, I often used to visit the store & interact with the customers to get their first hand insights on how they shop.

During one such interaction, I happened to assist a customer who had liked our stripped shirt and wanted to try it.

Me: Sir, this stripe shirt comes in two colored strips Black and Blue. Blue is one of our best sellers in this collection, would you like to try both and decide.

Customer- Yes give me both to try ON

Me: Sir, I would like you to these two shirts with a formal tie to see which one is more suited to you and uplift your professional dress etiquette. Please allow me to present you these two silk ties to try with these shirts.

Customer- yes, that make a good sense, bring it on.

If you notice the conversation that I was doing with the customer, I was not only assisting him but also adding value to his buying by suggesting him options as a professional personal shopper.

People love to be assisted when it comes to shopping garments.

They seek out for words which validates their buying decision. That is one of the reason why brick & mortar retail stores will always remain relevant even with facing an onslaught from ecommerce retailer.

Human interaction is impossible to replace.

If you walk into an Apple store, they have a tech bar concept with all geeks who are willing to help you with apple products and willing to answer all your queries.

At the apple store, I feel like a kid who experiences the same feeling when they visit an ice cream or candy store.

Personally, Love the way they make you to experience their products, no one disturbs you unless you ask for any assistance.

They encourage their customers to experience their products and then decide on their purchase. Infact post pandemic, in most of apple locations, one has to do pre-booking for visiting their stores as they are always crowded.

Apple stores organize regularly the classes for their customers wherein they share the tricks or hacks for operating their iPhone or MacBook's and learning the way to get more out of their machines.

This is one aspect which sets Apple apart from their competition.

They never force you to buy BUT you end up buying them as you fall in love.

Never Oversell yourself, your product or your brand.

Importance of meeting room and sitting configuration.

In B2B selling, it is very important as to how & where in the meeting room you sit with your prospect.

Always sit, adjacent to your prospect and not opposite to your prospect.

Body language and signs plays an important role in sales pitching process and thus in closing the sales.

Sitting opposite may subconsciously appear to be conflicting or confrontational whereas sitting adjacent to him will give a feeling of warmth and comfort. It communicates the same team spirit or camaraderie.

Closing is an outcome of a good presentation

During my tenure with one of the leading content creation studios, I used to make several presentations to various creative agencies and to their creative directors to showcase our strength in the production, postproduction and animations and special effects (these are terminologies used in advertising especially while making television commercials or web content videos for YouTube)

I often used to ask myself, "Am I in the business of making presentation or selling our services"

The answer was then revealed to me as a part of self-realization that until the customer was satisfied with our strengths in very specialized animation requirements, they would not assign us the project.

My sales objective was then transformed into understanding their requirements and then suggesting them the solutions in terms of presenting them the similar project works done internationally or solutions available to execute their requirements.

We combined animation with mobile i.e. by providing gamification ideas to brands wherein they could bring out their creative concept, not only in film but also by developing games, and further engaging their audience with the brand.

Marketers love customer engagement.

We transformed our basic showreel into problem solving mood boards and we presented live examples of film shot internationally using a similar platform or tools which our studio was specialized in executing.

If you notice, I had transformed myself from a sales manager into a SPECIALIST solution provider for my clients.

Change of this small technique proved a game changer for our agency as well since we were now able to charge a premium on our works since we were the only specialized animation studio in the region.

Digitalization of ABC principle of selling

In modern era of technology and social media, ABC principle is defined as "Always Be Communicating"

Build your lead generation channel

Lead Data is taken from a number of different sources and prospects are scored based on what they do on your website.

- Have they emailed you through Contact us page on your website?

- Have they interacted and asked your help in the WhatsApp group or social media pages.

Basically, identify from where the lead has come.

Start simple, by building a basic identity (persona) of what a customer looks like and identify prospects who look like that.

Your buyer persona is crucial, you need to define who are your prospects.

(I will discuss the creation of buyer's persona in the end of the book as a separate chapter)

Use consultative selling Shark salesman take a consultative approach – identifying their prospect's pain points first and tailoring their sales approach accordingly.

- Identify where a prospect is in the funnel.
- Is he a hot lead i.e. he has done his due diligence and ready to buy?
- Is he eager to know more about the product and its benefits?
- Is he simply here to learn more about your product n may buy in future?
- Or is he simply not interested in pursuing the discussion.

The trick to identifying the customer mindset is by asking him questions and then listening carefully and prompting him to disclose his true expectation from your product or service.

Build your community of customers.

Building trust is not a overnight game and takes time for the prospect to start trusting you and it may involve consistent communication with them.

Communication through

- Newsletters
- Retargeting of ads on social media
- Personalize emailers informing them about what's happening in your sector globally and how your brand can help them achieve or overcome their pain points.
- Hyper Personalisation tools are now available that help build a strong bond with customers.

Some tricks to help you close better.

- Post presentation, when you finish presenting and say thanks to your prospect for listening and asking question. It is always advisable to close it with a silence.

Don't push yourself to speak.
Stay calm, confident, and silent
Silence will put pressure on your prospect to speak up, either he would appreciate your presentation, or he would confront you with questions.

In both scenarios you win,

If the words are appreciative, you are closer to winning the pitch.

In case questions are asked, it signals that they are interested, and your presentation has done its task by aligning prospect's requirements.

You need then to answer their queries very diligently to close the sales.

Get rid of buyer's remorse

Buyer's remorse is nothing but a question that lingers in your customer's mind " I hope I made the right decision"

A shark salesman would follow up his sales order with a thank you note or email from his senior management to ensure the customer that they have made a right decision and you as an organization would ensure that the task get completed within the timelines set by the client.

Key take aways:

- Always remember that selling is a process of mutual consent with a common destination.
- Build your Lead Generation funnel.

Chapter 21

How to be a shark negotiator.

Negotiation is an important aspect of sales.

A salesman is regularly negotiating with customers either on Price, or with his Product teams on getting special offers for the customers.

In Retail, as a sales manager, you are negotiating with the malls /landlords for the rent reductions, better locations, better in-mall visibility, better high traffic footfall areas etc.

What is Negotiation?

It is a combination of Art & Science, a process wherein the disputes or differences are settled avoiding any legal hassles or arguments.

A good manager needs to be an accomplished Negotiator while dealing with his team members, interdepartmental heads, or his senior leadership.

Negotiation works on the principles of fairness, seeking mutual benefit, and maintaining a relationship are the keys to a successful negotiation outcome.

In this chapter, I shall narrate my learnings from the book "never split the difference" by author Chris Voss and what negotiation tips you must learn from Netflix web series "The Money heist" as it has some of the best negotiation scenes between authorities and banks robbers who took hostages in a bank robbery.

Effective Negotiation techniques

1) Using open-ended calibrated questions

It is one of the most potent tools in any negotiation process.

The questions to which the other side can respond but do not have specific or fixed answers.

It buys you time to think and strategize and at the same time gives the opposing party an illusion that they are in control of the talks.

2) Negotiation's technique can be effectively used in the corporate world wherein acquisition and mergers are the rules of the game.

3) Don't aim for "Yes" as an answer. Negotiation starts with "No".

One of the basic tenets of any negotiation is to separate the person & his emotions from the problem.

Don't focus on what the other side is asking, instead focus on their interests (why they are asking for it).

Work mutually for a win-win solution.

Establish mutually agreed-upon standards for evaluating those possible solutions.

- Emotions and emotional intelligence would have to be central to effective negotiation, and things to be overcome.
- Negotiation starts with the premise that people want to be understood and accepted.
- Listening skill is the cheapest and the most effective tool.
- By listening, a negotiator displays empathy and a sincere desire to better understand what the other side is experiencing.
- Ask calibrated questions that start with 'how' or 'what'. for example- How would you like me to proceed, what is it that brought us into this situation, How can we solve this standoff, etc.

Life is negotiation

The majority of the interactions we have at work or at home are negotiations that boil down to the expression of a simple, animalistic urge: "I Want".

Negotiation in its simplest form is nothing but effective communication.

Always establish your identity by giving your first name and designation to showcase you are responsible for taking this negotiation process forward and establishing rapport with the opponent.

Negotiation is asking the right thing.

Negotiation does not mean demeaning anyone or bowing down to someone's asks instead it is simply playing the emotional game.

In this world, you get what you ask for, you just have to ask it correctly.

In Negotiation – Be a mirror

One of the best qualities of a negotiator is that he makes the opponent talk, talk, and talk more about what they want.

Listening to their emotions and the "why" is the most crucial.

Voice modulation

The most powerful tool in any communication is your voice.

When we radiate warmth, understanding, acceptance, the conversations just seem to flow.

Smile at someone and they smile back as a reflex action. Understanding this trick is the core to successful negotiations.

Listen to the late-night FM channel and see how the RJ talks over the radio, with his calming voice that soothes you and takes away all the tensions. Practice talking in a calming tone when you are dealing with any negotiation process.

Mirroring – a negotiation technique

It is also our natural instinct when we imitate others to calm them down and establish some kind of connection or trust.

Salesman uses this technique effectively while making their sales pitch.

Neutralize the negative and reinforce the positive.

People's emotions have two levels –

"the presenting" behavior wherein you can see and hear.

Beneath, the **"underlying"** feeling is what motivates that behavior.

Imagine an old grandfather, who is cranky at the dinner table, but his underlying emotion is that he is fighting with the feeling of loneliness.

If you address the underlying feeling, you would have comforted the old man and won his trust.

The same rationale works in any kind of negotiation process.

Practice Empathy

The beauty of empathy is that it doesn't demand that you agree with the other person's ideas but by acknowledging the other person's situation, you immediately convey that you are listening.

And once your opponent knows that you are listening, they may tell you something which you can use.

How to make a person respond to your emails and not ignore you?

You have been following up with some client prospect of yours and there is no acknowledgment nor any response from their end.

The best trick is to provoke a 'No' with this one-sentence email.

"Have you given up on this project?"

This question demands the other party to define their position and explain it to you.

There is a high probability of getting your client to say 'yes' to your offer.

Negotiation skill demands Practice, Practice, and Practice.

When the pressure is on, you don't rise to the occasion, you fall to your highest level of preparation.

So be consistent in practicing this skill set.

Chapter 22

Managing expectations

Most of the conflicts in the world arises since we don't manage the expectations of the aggrieved opposite party.

In your sales career, you will come across angry customers and you need to manage them and earn their respect and trust.

The question is, how to handle angry customers?

Speaking from my experience, you allow the customer to talk and Vent out all his anger so the best way to manage an angry customer is by allowing him/her to vent out their frustrations.

Never argue or interrupt the customer as they will get defensive and you may lose the customer forever.

Practice Empathy.

Listen to them while they shout to understand what part of the process caused so much frustrations in them.

- Was it defective product? Or wrong product shipped to them?

- Was it late delivery of the good?
- Was it faulty payment process?

Let the customer speak out the core reason for their frustrations or anger.

Never take it Personal

While the customer is shouting at you, you need to stay calm and never take any word personally.

Understand that the customer is expressing his anger towards your company and not to you as an individual.

From my personal experience, let me tell you that my best friends today, were my most aggrieved customers in the past.

"Great relationship starts with a fight" was one of the lines that I had read in some book in the past and it remained stuck on me.

Give your customer Respect while they are angry with the services, ask politely as what can you do to meet their expectations.

Most conflicts arises when expectations are not met.

Ways to manage expectations:

- Create experience with expectation i.e set the expectations in the first place.

What do you expect when you drive Ford Mustang?

I am sure you will say, Thrill, Power , more macho, adventures.

You try to set expectations which are linked to experiences and your goal as a salesman to ensure that those experiences fulfill the desired expectations.

- Advertising companies always play of the art of creating expectations through their persuasive creative campaigns.

For example, take an advertisement of any detergent brand, they all talk about the power of cleaning the stains from your clothes and leaving them as fresh as new.

But one of the unilever's brand communicates that "stains are good".

It brings people together to enjoy festivities, spirit of togetherness, ignore the stains aside, for which unilever's detergent is there to take care. They persuade consumers to engage themselves in the spirit of togetherness, good deeds and forget about stains on their clothes.

Different expectations and prior knowledge can lead to very different perceptions of the same product (in above example detergent)

Another example that comes to my mind is from tea manufacturer, Tata tea (popular tea in India)

While all their competition were shouting for "freshness" , "stronger tea blends"; Tata tea came up with the persuasive campaign called " Jago India" (awake India)

They raised the issues like literacy for all, growth for domestics industries , women empowerment and other social topics.

The result was fantastic for the brand in terms of recall & immediate acceptance.

People related themselves with the brand's communication.

Key take away

No body likes to be sold. People are interested in them. If you can persuade them towards you with your compelling story then you have won the people's heart.

One of the best way to manage expectations is through Persuasive communication.

A shark salesman need to talk about what the customer wants.

When we stop trying to change what people want and instead try to show people, how to get what they want.

We bring the difference in our communication strategy.

How to manage expectations at work?

Most of us spend one-third of our life at work or at job.

Most of the employee's dissatisfaction or low morale is due non-management of expectations which results in high employee turnover.

How to avoid it?

- Have a candid talk with your immediate manager or line manager and ask him/her as to what are their expectations from you.
- Listen carefully while your line manager talks, Listen for cues of improvement in the dept, listen for hidden expectations.
- (bottom line in corporate world, make your Boss look good in front of the stakeholders and you shall thrive in the organization)
- Set out clear expectation and document it with your line manager
- Work out a plan as to how you will set to accomplish each expectation.
- Share your plan with you line manager and incorporate his views.
- Translate the expectation into achievable goals.
- Action the Goals as per the timelines set.

Always remember there are two things in life that you cannot choose

a) Your parents
b) Your Boss/Manager

Hence setting a clearly defined expectations and goals in the beginning of your role will help you manage expectations strongly and effectively.

Remember, like you are seeking a good boss, a boss is also seeking a good subordinate.

"what you are seeking, is also seeking you"

When you always deliver or give more than what you are getting paid for, you shall never have to bother about your career development. This is one of the law of attraction.

Just try to get better at getting better.

Chapter 23

Customer's Personas

Today we all are in digital arena and hence Selling skills also need to adapt to technological advancements.

Knowing who are your customers or your prospects is crucial wherein the most of selling and marketing is done online.

Sales people constantly are looking for leads (hot or warm) to sell their products & services (especially in B2B kind of business).

We also call it as Lead generation.

Social media can be leveraged to generate leads for your businesses (especially Linkedin).

The critical requirement is to know who your ideal prospect or customer and their personas is.

Once you know about your customer personas, you'll be able to attract high-value visitors, leads, and customers to your business who you'll be more likely to retain over time.

Moreover, know your customer persona will help you develop content creation in order to communicate with them and add value to them, will help you in product development, sales follow up, and really *anything* that relates to customer acquisition and retention.

How to create Buyer's personas?

You can create your buyer's personas using Interests, i.e. targeting your content message to those who share similar interests.

- Based on preferences i.e. those customers who prefers and have affinity towards your product or services.
- Based on geography & events.
- Relook at your existing customers and prospective customers databases and put them into blocks named " Hot leads" and "warm leads" & "cold leads"
- In case you are using retargeting tools, then you need strategies your sales communication separately targeting to each segment.
- For example, for warm leads, you can communicate current promotions to entice them to buy your services. You can offer exclusive previews or demos or free subscriptions period to Hot leads in order to retain them in your business.

One of the most critical steps to establishing your buyer persona(s) is finding some people to speak with to validate who your buyer persona is.

That means you'll have to conduct some interviews to get to know what drives your target audience.

1. Use your current customers.

Your existing customer base is the perfect place to start with your interviews because they've already purchased your product and engaged with your company. At least some of them are likely to exemplify your target persona(s).

Don't just talk to people who love your product and want to spend an hour gushing about you (as good as that feels).

Customers who are unhappy with your product will show other patterns that will help you form a solid understanding of your personas.

For example, you might find that some of your *less*happy customers have bigger teams and need greater collaboration functionality from your product. Or, you may find they find your product too technical and difficult to use. In both cases, you learn something about your product and what your customers' challenges are.

Another benefit to interviewing current customers is that you may not need to offer them an incentive (e.g. gift card) to do so.

Customers often like being heard — interviewing them gives them a chance to tell you about their world, their challenges, and what they think of your product.

Customers also like to have an impact on the products they use. So, as you involve them in interviews like this, you may find they become even more loyal to your company.

When you reach out to customers, be clear that your goal is to get their feedback, and that their feedback is highly-valued by your team.

2. Use your prospects.

Be sure to interview people who have not purchased your product and don't know much about your brand, too. Your current prospects and leads are a great option here because you already have their contact information.

Use the data you do have about them (i.e. anything you've collected through lead generation forms or website analytics) to figure out who might fit into your target personas.

Use your referrals.

The best way is to ask your existing customers to refer you to someone in their network whom they feel that your product or service could also provide value.

In digital marketing we call this as a affiliate marketing wherein the referee gets some percentage for providing referral upon closing of sales.

Use your network — such as your coworkers, existing customers, social media contacts — to find people you'd like to interview and be introduced to. It may be tough to get a large volume of people this way, but you'll likely get some very high-quality interviews out of it.

If you don't know where to start, try searching on LinkedIn for people who may fit into your target personas and see which results have any connections in common with you.

Use ad forms.

This is an effective way to generate some interested warm leads from your prospects wherein you target your advertisement asking them to fill out their information in case they want to know more about your product or demo and in return, you offer them a secured seat in your upcoming free webinar or eBook as a good gesture.

> The Best prospect is the client who has already dealt with you. The second best is the one referred to by a client who has dealt with you previously. The third best is the one referred to you by another trusted professional or friend.

Build your own lead gen engine

The success of a salesman is directly proportional to the effectiveness of the network he has built.

We get tied down to daily tasks that we forget this important aspect of building your own network.

Salesmen are like Karna (the mythological character in Mahabharata, a distinguished archer), he was punished by his teacher to whom he had once lied. The curse given to Karna was that he would forget his guru's teaching at the time when he most required it.

We in sales don't realize our true weapon is the database or network that we create.

Tips for networking.

A) Start networking with your established network.

B) Don't expect any business in the beginning. Invest in networking for building TRUST amongst your network.

C) Give & add value to your network by constantly being visible and giving valuable content or information about the sector of your business.

D) Maintain and grow your network through the use of social media

Don't sell till you develop Trust and creditability amongst your network as "GO TO" person.

Shark salesman understand the reaction towards any COLD Calling is always Cold.

Engage with your network through calls, meetups, whatsapp, direct mailers etc.

In case you want to reach out to a prospect in a new organization you are pitching, it is highly probable to check for any reference with your network first since someone in your network would have prior connections in the organization that you are trying to reach and a quick call to them would help you secure a meeting with your prospect.

Hence leveraging the power of your network is crucial in running business in digital age.

A quick tip to find out the interests of your prospect.

Never ask or say, "what do you do in your free time", instead ask "How do you spend your day or time".

Watch out for the reply, if the prospect say, " I work most of the times means your invitations for dinner or lunch would be declined". But incase he says, " I maintain time between work and leisure" then he would positively respond to your request for a dinner or quick drinks.

Chapter 24

Quick hacks to incorporate in your selling

This is the last chapter of the book and I am going to list down few tricks and hacks that you can incorporate in your selling pitch immediately to stand out from the rest of the salesman.

Hack 1: Never say "thank you" alone.

Always tie thank you with a word, for instance

"thank you for coming"

"thank you for listening to me patiently"

"thank you for waiting"

"Thank you for asking"

Saying "thank you" alone will make people lose its relevancy.

In order to be heard, you need to tie it up with word.

"Thank you for getting us to a team building event boss" will be more relevant to your boss instead of a plain "thank you"

Hack 2 : How to get insider's information?

Dale Carnegie, gives out this hack.

"show sincere interest in people and people will talk"

By asking intelligent questions, you can make people open up and present their thoughts to you in a candid manner.

Hack 3: People love to do business with People they like.

It has been proven that people are most receptive to those they feel have the same values in life.

The quote " Birds of a feather flock together" holds true in sales as well.

Hence networking becomes crucial for the modern age sales professionals.

We are most comfortable giving our business and friendship to those we feel share our values and beliefs in life.

Hack 4: Be lavish in your praise.

People love to be acknowledged and praised.

Throw few comments in your conversation to praise the person with whom you are talking to.

It helps building rapport and trust.

"You have a wonderful air about your honesty"

Hack 5 : always ask "Is it a good time to call"

When you ask about the timing first, there is a high probability that you will never get a "No". Try it and check it for yourself.

Hack 6: How to work a party like a politician works a room

In his book " how to talk anyone" the author leil lowdnes narrates this concept which I feel can add value to a sales professional.

A shark salesman learns the trick from a politician.

A politician prior to accepting a party invite will do his home-work by asking the following questions.

-Who is going to be at the party? Whom should I meet at the party who can help me achieve my goals or provide me leads?

- When should I arrive? If the party is going to full of corporate leaders then I should be on time and meet & greet with corporate leaders and exchange their cards.

- Why party is being given? Is it a networking event or award function? Is the party a specific industry event?

- How am I going to follow up post the party? A good politician ensures that he sends a short note to the person met stating "with compliments" and know when he need to call upon in case he needs any industry specific information.

A shark salesman should adopt these qualities when he is planning to attend any networking event.

Few observations and tricks go a long way in building connections and network.

Chapter 25

Leadership In selling.

Sales is all about managing People (sales teams) and customers.

You as a shark salesman need to be proficient in managing customer's expectations and leveraging your leadership skills to get the task done by your team.

Managing People is the most difficult task since I strongly believe that People cannot be managed.

Being a father, try managing your kids for a day and you will soon realize they don't even care for what you are asking them to do.

Forget managing others.

People can only be inspired and get them aligned with your corporate vision, followed by giving a free hand to them to perform the task.

As a shark salesman, you can get your people to motivate themselves.

Motivation if injected is short lived but when it comes from within it creates magic.

> Leadership is the art of getting someone else to do something you want done because he wants to do it.
>
> -   Dwight D Eisenhower

A shark sales leader never focuses on telling his team " How to do" instead he communicates to his team " what needs to be done" and provide the requisite tools and environment for the team to deliver on the tasks.

Trick is understanding and knowing each member of your team.

One of the challenges that I had personally encountered was an average sales performance from some of my team members.

Average sales performer would only do what is required is bare minimum required from them, they will never push themselves to push the limits.

This average performance mentality is the result from their past behaviors and beliefs (especially due to our education system – we need only passing percentage in order to finish graduation, forget about getting distinctions or topping in the exams).

In order to correct this behaviour, I got some of my best performing team mates to give and conduct hands-on , on-shop (on-site) training and mentoring to these average performers.

We implemented the gamification aspect to coaching wherein the senior member used to coach the other salesman in the store and if the trainee salesman sells more than the daily required average then we used to give them a special badge every day.

The game was to collect the maximum number of badges to receive cash awards including air tickets to your home country and town.

By introducing gamification in sales, I solved two things.

- Made the average performer realize that we need to go beyond daily required average.
- Made them aware that going beyond the desired average sales is possible and they have done it and can do it again. (self-awareness and self-realization).

Sales Leader always give Feedback.

We as human beings love to be acknowledged and crave for feedback or recognition from our peers.

You would have noticed a small kid, in order to get the attention of his parents, he/she will first make some funny noises and moves but if there is no reaction or appreciation, the baby would start crying.

The same thing applies when it comes to motivate People.

Giving feedback and acknowledging their efforts goes a long way in developing your team and yourself as a People's Manager.

Be lavish in your praise always and give feedback to every member of your team irrespective of how insignificant the task was.

The managers who have the biggest trouble motivating their people are the ones who give the least feedback.

Achieving sales targets requires continuous feedback.

Listening to your team, getting their suggestions, making them feel heard and important are all important aspect of sales leaderships.

If you are heading a sales function of Retail organization then, ask your sales team questions like:

- How can we make buying process more interesting for our customers?
- How can we ensure that once they enter the shop, they leave with a big smile?
- How can we motivate the store sales team and celebrate even small wins?
- How do we get the store team more involved in the success of the store?

A shark salesman will show his leadership skill by continuously asking these questions and actioning on the suggestions received from the team.

> It is not the "will to win" that wins the game. Instead, it is "the will to prepare to win"

Be inspiring.

Words are the world's most powerful weapons.

A shark sales leader knows this fact and chooses his words very effectively and efficiently.

As once Mahatma Gandhi said, " You can't change People. You must be the change you wish to see in people".

Lead from the front.

As a sales leader you need to lead from front and set examples for your team mates.

Clear communication of goals and sales team KPI (key performance Indicators) are the key to achieve bigger goals.

As a sales leader, you must be lethal in communication goals and what is expected from your team members.

You should know when to motivate them and when to the pull the plugs.

Giving feedback is a form of communicating with your team mates.

Focus on " want to do" rather than " How to do" task.

A sales leader always communicates as to why the task is relevant for the individual salesman. What benefit will it bring to them; How they would become more productive with the same kind of inputs;

People are interested in "what's in for me" concept.

You need to align their aspirations with your sales goals and orient your sales team to believe that the set objectives can be achieved by them. The Buy-In from the sales team is critical for the sales generation.

Good sales management is outcome management.

A good sales leader teaches his team mates to become more accountable and take ownership for their behaviors and actions which will lead them to become a better human being.

> The best executive is the one who has sense enough to pick good people to do what he wants done, and self-restraint to keep from meddling with them while they do it.
>
> - Theodore Roosevelt.

Reference Books:

How to talk to anyone – by leil Lowndes.

A salesman's lessons – by C R jena

Delivering Happiness – by Tony Hsieh

Catalyst – by Chandramouli Venkatesan

The leader who had no title – by Robin sharma

100 great sales ideas – by Patrick Forsyth

7 secrets of Persuasion – by James Crimmins

You can sell – by Shiv khera

100 ways to motivate others – Steve Chandler and Scott Richardson.